Fren

Keep &

Fr. Martin Connor κ

Christmas 2014

MW00975678

10 Reflections on the Kingdom

Insights into the Spirituality of Regnum Christi

Father Martin Connor, LC

TABLE OF CONTENTS

At the Close of the *Year of the Faith* 2013

The fruits of the Second Vatican Council speak through the Catholic Church's new ecclesial movements in new and unique ways. This collection of essays tries to offer insight into the spirit of the Movement Regnum Christi as it gives new perspective to the Christian understanding of Kingdom.

Jesus said: "The Kingdom of God is like…"
(Mk 4,26)

Dedication

When people ask how my vocation came about, how this whole "priesthood thing" happened, I tend to give the same answer. I don't really know. It's not always what you think. Vocations come in all shapes and sizes. The fact is that the first rumblings of any calling in me were not specifically to the priesthood, but rather sounded like this: "you are going to be part of a family that wants to do something great for God." The charismatic family of the Regnum Christi Movement,[1] which includes the Legion of Christ, *is* that family, and it changed my life over twenty years ago.

The phenomenon of ecclesial movements, like Regnum Christi, in the Catholic Church, is something from the last 100 years though similar moments of renewal have happened in Church's history. These ecclesial movements are new spiritual families that enrich our Catholic faith and seek to bring all to Christ. The new movements are Catholic and experience a unity of purpose, yet each movement's spirit is a unique expression of Divine Love. They have produced many spiritual and apostolic fruits, showing themselves, in the words of St. John Paul II, as "one of the Spirit's gifts to our times." They manifest a new missionary advent, a great "Christian springtime prepared by God at the threshold of the third millennium of the Redemption."[2]

I write these reflections to the many faithful and committed followers of Christ in the ranks of the charismatic family Regnum Christi who have stayed the course through the difficult and trying times we have faced in our history. Thank you for your steadfast love and faith in this work of God. It is *His* work. These reflections serve only to confirm you in what you already know and love about your spiritual family. I write also to the men and women of our present culture who will be touched by the *charism resonance* in these few pages. It is Christ who calls and sends us. And with his grace we respond. May these reflections give you the courage to respond to whatever he is calling you to do.

Acknowledgements

My gratitude goes out to the many who had even a finger in the collaborative effort of this book especially the following: Sarah Sullivan, Fr David Daly LC, Evelyn Auth, Kathy Knopka, Fr John Connor LC, Monica Oppermann, Br Christopher Gronotte LC, Marcia Silvestro, Isaf family, Fr Patrick Langan LC, Janet McLaughlin, Fr Javier Fayos LC, Serge Sautre, Fr Michael Luxbacher LC, Melissa Foley, and Fernanda Paez.

Expressions of the Kingdom: Unity and Charity

Every kingdom divided against itself will be ruined, and every city or household divided against itself will not stand...Whoever is not with me is against me, and whoever does not gather with me scatters.   *(Mt. 12:25, 30)*

Unity is a work of love. Love is by its very nature a builder not a divider. The Holy Spirit is the great builder in us and in our communities because He is the unique expression of the love between the Father and the Son sent to us by Christ himself at the end of his earthly life: "I will ask the Father and he will give you another advocate to be with you forever" (John 14:16). Regnum Christi acknowledges Him as the builder of her unity, which is essential to the effectiveness of her apostolic mission. Unity is critical when trying to build a family or community in one direction – a single direction towards God; and, it is tragic to see so many families and communities in the Church torn apart by disunity. "Every kingdom divided against itself will be ruined, and every city or household divided against itself will not stand" (Matthew 12:25). This is certainly not the work of the Spirit, but rather the work of the evil one who sows discord and stifles the Spirit through indifference and selfishness. In the final analysis, the true and greatest enemy of the Christian is selfishness and resistance to true faith in the Gospel. [3]The Regnum Christi Movement wants to be a leaven of renewal to combat these enemies and is called to live an intense unity fueled by love within its own body. Only through the Holy Spirit, the transcendent protagonist behind every work of holiness and apostolate in every person and in the entire world, will this be possible.

Within a given spiritual family in the Church, like Regnum Christi, the "glue" of the unity is called the charism. St. John Paul II noted this when he said that the secret, so to speak, is found in the charisms which have produced the movements and which constitute their very soul. It is the charism which produces the "spiritual affinity between individuals" animating a community and a movement. Thanks to this charism, the original experience of the Christian reality can be re-lived and re-produced in the lives of many people and of many generations of people without losing its novelty and freshness...the charism is also the source of the extraordinary educating power of the movements.[4] Hence it is imperative that we interiorize the spirit of our family, by knowing and living its charism so it can then be transmitted as a gift of God to the Church with our very lives. The formation received in Regnum Christi allows for this interiorization; a formation whose departure point is a deep conversion of heart. The conversion is lived as a free gift of God, a gift that fills the heart with joy and becomes a spiritual benefit for the whole of one's life. No longer distant and aloof from my daily reality, God becomes something for me, even better *someone* to me. Each of the new Movements in the Church bases its formative process [of the person] on a distinct, specific pedagogical approach which is typically Christ-centered. It focuses on what is truly essential, which is the awakening in the person of that baptismal vocation or identity that characterizes true Christian discipleship. It is radical in the sense that it refuses to dilute the Gospel by proposing holiness as an ideal worthy to be pursued.[5]

Even beyond formation is the *communion of persons* that is found among those living the charism. A communion of persons is created when two or more persons give themselves to one another in love. This communion or unity is deeper than just mere external appearances of a common spirituality or education in the faith. Pope Francis touches on this when he says "our faith exists as part of a dialogue and cannot be merely a profession originating in an individual...this openness to the ecclesial "We" reflects the openness to Gods own love."[6] Unity is a work of love. Love builds. Thus, within this spiritual family, it is a priority to create esteem for one another and for all people, to be merciful towards the defects of our brothers and sisters, to ponder and promote the good qualities and virtues they possess, and to share the successes and failures they have. Yet, we are called to be our brother's keeper. We do need to admonish our brothers, where necessary, precisely because they *are* our brothers, as we would our own family who struggle in life.

The basic reason that we admonish our brothers is because their salvation is the greatest good and need in their lives and may well be in jeopardy. If a person was drowning, and we were standing near a life preserver, and we did not throw him some help, this would be a gross lack of love. The same goes for our spiritual health. The letter to the Hebrews insists on this: "Do not refuse [the one] who is speaking. For if they did not escape when they refused him who warned them on earth, much less shall we escape if we reject him who warns from heaven" (Heb 12:25). Such sincere caring for one another is the catalyst for a profound communion and a true family spirit, one that desires to live the call received from Christ faithfully.

Questions for Group Discussion:

1. What ways can I build others up and not tear them down? How do I ask for the intercession of the Holy Spirit in times of weakness in this regard?

2. How do I work on my individual formation? What are some of the fruits of catholic my formation that have brought me closer to God? Do I have a plan for my ongoing formation in the faith?

3. How and when do I work with others in the Church, in the Movement? How might I better support others in times of need? How do I challenge others to live our faith to the fullest?

Chapter II

What does "Kingdom" mean?

*The Kingdom of heaven is like a mustard seed....It is the
smallest of all the seeds, yet when full-groan, it is the largest of
plants. It becomes a large bush, and the birds of the sky come
and dwell in its branches.*   *(Mt 13:31-32)*

What does it mean when our Lord tells us his
"Kingdom is not of this world," (John 18:36)? Could
He mean 'otherworldly' as in not of our
material/earthly world? Our world is one in which the
material is paramount and the *spiritual* is not
recognized. Our culture seems to say, "if I cannot see
it, touch it, taste it, or smell it, then it has no meaning
for me, no immediate value, and it is dismissed
because of its perceived lack of importance. The
spiritual and the material seem to be, at best, divided
and appear to be different worlds. Yet the Kingdom
of God, revealed to us by the gift of Christ's coming,
is a unification of the spiritual and the material. Our
world is a fallen world, separated from God by sin,
and Christ (who is fully human and fully Divine), has
come to heal our fallen world by offering to us his
very self. God has chosen to allow this Kingdom, this
new world, to reside within each human being just as
he did when he first created life. "God breathed into
his nostrils the breath of life and the man became a

living being." (Gen 2:7) The Kingdom is the "breathing in" of God a second time with new life.

The Kingdom affects all of us, but in particular our very spirits. Six months after my ordination to the priesthood, my father died. When I went to see the body of my dead father in the morgue, and the sheet was removed, yes, it was his body, but, it was *not* him. My father was not there because his spiritual soul was not there. The *soul* "refers to the innermost aspect of man, that which is of greatest value in him, that by which he is most especially in God's image; the *soul* signifies the *spiritual principle* in man."[1] It was clear to me in that moment at the morgue that we are not just a material body but truly body and soul, a living unity. So the Kingdom is about all of me but begins with what is inside of me. I cannot see it and touch it. Jesus said this himself, "the Kingdom of God is within you" (Luke 17:21).

We begin with Jesus's own words: *The Kingdom of God is within you.* Perhaps in more simple terms, we could define the Kingdom as an interior openness to the action of God which beckons me to respond *first* in selfless love to all human experiences. This inner disposition is literally "born" or initiated in baptism when the seed of divine life through the gifts of faith, hope and charity are sown in my soul by the Holy Spirit. Jesus uses the image of the action of yeast in dough to explain (cf. Mt. 13:33). Anyone who likes to bake knows that yeast has the ability to permeate an entire mass of dough causing it to grow, multiply and change its very shape. The yeast is that divine seed sown in Baptism. It is infused divine life in me, which changes me, and transforms my spirit.

Now, this change in me does not happen immediately. After Baptism, we are disposed by grace (God's *power* in us) to love in this way because God's divine spirit now dwells with us. Jesus promised this: "we will come to you and make our abode in you" (John 14:23). The yeast that transforms the dough reflects the action of grace, an action that is not visible through human eyes and that works invisibly, through prayer, the reception of the sacraments, small deeds and events. Yeast transforms dough for bread in the same way that the spiritual life transforms a man. The yeast of the spirit transforms man and converts him into a citizen of the Kingdom of Heaven. So, the Kingdom truly does begin within each of us. A baptized Christian person who accepts the grace of God with an open spirit transforms his life. When my interior way of being becomes more Christ-like, more divine-like, with the help of this new power called grace, then I will not wait to be loved by others, but I will respond *first* in love like Christ did. This is what God did, He loved us first (cf. 1 John 4, 20) and now it's our turn with His help. This fact alone -- living from the very spirit of God himself – of carrying Christ inside - should move us to be unafraid in our loving, ready to love even the unlovable.

With all this said, let us have one thing very clear in our minds. This change in us is the *pure gift* of God. In a world so immersed in individualism and personal autonomy with the evident loss of awareness that we are wholly dependent on an *Other* for salvation, that Other who is Almighty God, how easy it is to gradually transfer our confidence to things or to self. In his letters to the first Christians, St. Paul is insistent in his warning of this danger and to one such a community he says: "For who sees anything different in you? What have you that you did not receive? If then you received it, why do you boast as if it were not a gift?"(1 Cor 4:7) For the sake of the world and for our own sake, as individuals and as Church-- not to mention anyone who is part of a new spiritual family in the Church-- we desperately need not to behave as if what we have in the way of spiritual and material goods is due to our own merit or a result of our own will or strength. There should be a resounding "No!" to this way of thinking. It is the pure grace of God. All of what we have and who we are is the pure grace of God and is meant to be given back to Him in our acts of love, big and small.

Through Regnum Christi, like many new movements in the Church, "many people have met Christ for the first time and believed in him or have returned to the Church and the sacraments after years of being away. So many people have gone from being Christians in name only to believers who are convinced and committed."[2] Yet, at the same time, Regnum Christi is an *apostolic* movement. Over and over, her members speak of the call to Regnum Christi as being a call to deepen their commitment to Christ, just as the early apostles were called forth to a total commitment of life and love for the work of their Savior. The Greek word *apostello* means "to send forth," or "to dispatch."[3]

The "Kingdom" has an interior and exterior expression; our spirituality refers to it as *contemplative and evangelizing*. Just as this divine action begins growing in me, so too does it need to happen to others in our world *through me*. We should be *intentional* for this to happen even anxious, but not overbearingly anxious. A follower of Christ has to be just like the yeast in the dough that makes bread rise and provide more, by being the yeast that makes Christ's message spread wherever he is, at home or work or school, with friends and all those around him. So we can say that the Kingdom is made present when the gifts of faith, hope and love (divine life in me) permeate the whole of society through individuals. From the tiny seed that God planted in my soul one day in baptism, a large tree will grow and many friends will look for shade and shelter under it; that is, they will look for friendship and my company because I will transmit something that they don't have. Again, Jesus promises it: *The Kingdom of God is like a mustard seed....it is the smallest of seeds but when it has grown it is the biggest shrub of all and becomes a tree so that the birds of the air come and shelter in is branches"* (Mt 13: 31-32). The experience of Christ can only be transmitted by someone who has had that encounter. It is obtained little by little by knowing Christ and learning to love him.

For those called to live this evangelizing dimension of the spirituality of Regnum Christi, someone who carries Christ inside is not capable of keeping him in. He gives off Christ like perfume even when he isn't trying to, in fact the more natural it is the better! It is the realization of the need to become a living cell in the body of Christ (the Church) that continually tries to transform every atmosphere and to attract abundant new cells for Christ. Regnum Christi is not just its teams or its formation. The Movement is its members, it is *you*. It is *you* who want to respond to Christ's friendship in a real way, by being a living cell and the yeast that ferments the dough of your environment.[4] Jesus uses that powerful image of yeast to explain the Kingdom of God, where faith and true charity are called to permeate the secular world and make Christ reign in the hearts and minds of all men.

Yet, where there is good, there will be that which spoils the good. In the Gospel, Jesus warns us of bad leaven: the leaven of the Pharisees, pride, and that of Herod, sensuality. He warns us to be vigilant so that pride and sensuality do not take root in our hearts to poison it. We are summoned to battle against this bad leaven, countering it with an active faith and authentic Gospel charity. St. Paul knows of this type of bad yeast when he speaks to the Ephesians, highlighting nevertheless the power of their personal witness: "Be careful about the sort of lives you lead, like intelligent and not like senseless people. This may be a wicked age, but *your lives should redeem it*" (cf. Ephesians 5:15). What a responsibility we have not to squander this gift that he entrusts to us, to give it freely and joyfully to others and embrace with gratitude the call to participate and partner with God in this divine project of redeeming souls.

Questions for Group Discussion:

1. How well do I respond to God's call to love? What concrete ways do I both love God and others, especially the "unlovable" in my life?

2. What intentional actions do I take to allow God to grow in me? How is this growth attracting others to Christ?

3. How am I vigilant to the wicked pulls of the world on my heart? How do I battle this "bad leaven" with my faith and authentic Gospel charity?

Chapter III

Establishing the Kingdom of Christ

*The Regnum Christi Movement proposes a Christian way of
life...rather than adding new commitments, it helps its
members to live those that derive from their baptism. Far
from being an additional demand to fit in alongside their
marriage, family and social duties, it offers its members a
unifying vehicle to live these duties in the conviction that
through them they fulfill their mission of being Christian
leaven in the world. (*Regnum Christi Member Handbook, *no. 20)*

There is no question that we are living in
unprecedented times in human history, times of
terrible moral persecutions, within the fortress of
Mother Church, outside her walls, as well as
spiritual attacks on people of goodwill in all areas
of society. The pontificate of Pope Francis seems
to confirm the consistency of the Holy Spirit in its
continual calling for renewal in the Church, a
renewal that begins by returning to the foundations
of our baptism – to "remember our first love" (Rev
2:4). As an ecclesial movement called to be leaven
to a "war-torn" culture, to bring this authentic
spiritual renewal out in to the culture, Regnum
Christi exists to help others weather these storms,
storms that as we all can attest, begin in the heart of
every man and woman. We must remember, as
our recent history has shown us, that our very
existence as a movement of the Holy Spirit within

the loving arms of the Catholic Church, comes from this call to renewal.

Regnum Christi Movement aspires to establish Christ's Kingdom. This is what first inspired the work of the Legionaries of Christ, and subsequently all of Regnum Christi. It appears in one of the first drafts of the Legionary Constitutions and is the central idea in every aspect of legionary life, that is, the preaching and establishment of the Kingdom of Christ as the ideal that inspires, stimulates, and directs the apostolic ends of the religious community. If the establishment of the Kingdom of Christ is the primordial task of any member of Regnum Christi, what does it mean exactly "to establish the Kingdom?" It can be summed up in one word: love.

God who is love became a man. The source of all love was *enfleshed* in a person, in Jesus Christ. The Regnum Christi Movement's mission consists in bringing the greatest number of people *to know God's love* deeply, as the ultimate explanation of the redemption wrought by Christ; in bringing them *to live in love* by practicing the authentic and generous charity Christ preached and demanded; and, finally, in striving *to make God's merciful love known* to all mankind by tirelessly preaching the gospel, so as to achieve the conversion of hearts and build a civilization of Christian justice and love."[1]

To establish the Kingdom is to teach Christ by giving Christ. To give Christ is to teach that love is a choice, the choice of making yourself a gift to the other rather than using another as a means for some pleasure or end, which is so very common in our world. Ultimately, love is a choice for Good over Evil. To establish the Kingdom of Christ is to establish a consistency of choice in one's life, the choice to reject sin and to do good out of love, to imitate Jesus Christ who "went about doing good." (Acts 10:38) To do this, we begin by repenting of anything that separates us from God. This is why perhaps Christ begins his mission with "the Kingdom of God is at hand" and then went on to say "repent and believe" (Mk 1:15). *Incarnate Love sees sin as the greatest evil in the world and the greatest obstacle to love.* "To the eyes of faith no evil is graver than sin and nothing has worse consequences for sinners themselves, for the Church, and for the whole world"[2].

Truthfully, however, much of the time we are reluctant to even try change our ways because we feel so helpless, so weak. We shrink back because of shame and regret of past choices. We lose hope. Yet, with these words of Christ "repent and believe," it was like he was saying, "there is something new happening here, listen up, you don't have to take the path that you are currently on, don't be content with where you are if you are unhappy, there exists another way, a way that will lead to true fulfillment but you need to change your ways." You need to change your heart. Later in the Gospel, Christ says the "Kingdom of God is upon you" (Matthew 12:28). Words uttered precisely in relation to evil, to the turning away from evil, in rejecting the power of Satan. To receive true love we need to turn away from the enemy of love and receive forgiveness.

Christ links the Kingdom intimately to the forgiveness of sins: "repent and believe." St. Paul iterates the same to some of the first Christians: "Because what Christ has done: he has taken us out of the power of darkness and created a place for us in the kingdom of the Son that he loves, and in him, we gain our freedom, the forgiveness of our sins" (Col 1:13-14). With sin, we were cut off from God and cast into a spiritual darkness. Through the sacrifice of Christ on the cross, *everyone* is undeservedly offered the gift of redemption by God. "The paschal mystery, Christ's dying and rising, is the definitive victory of the Kingdom of God over the kingdom of sin and death".[3] In a sense, when we speak of establishing the Kingdom, we refer to the announcing of God's love and mercy, to the announcing of the true *freedom* that Jesus Christ desires for us, to allowing Him to break the bonds of sin in our lives and to cast out the darkness in our spirit.

In order for a person to be free to love, he or she must be free from internal constraint. Internal constraint involves the tendency we have to use another for our selfish desires. Only if a person is freed from this tendency is he or she really able to love another. Just as the desire to love can be disordered and manifested as lust, the desire for freedom can be disordered and manifested in slavery. St. Paul spoke of the danger of this slavery to the early Christians: "You, my brothers and sisters, were called to be free. But do not use your freedom to indulge the flesh; rather, serve one another humbly in love." (Galatians 5:13) If you are not free to control your own desires, how can you be free to love? Being free to love is only possible through the grace of God who gives us pure hearts. Once we choose God and allow His grace to transform our desires, then *the moral life becomes a life not about rules, but about love.*[4] This is what the spirit of Christ's love and mercy gives to each of us: "Now the Lord is the Spirit, and where the Spirit of the Lord is, there is freedom" (2 Corinthians 3:17). If establishing Christ's

Kingdom is exposing people to this freedom, then we should rightfully exclaim "Thy Kingdom Come!" In a world so often consumed with false notions of freedom, this is truly the Gospel, the good news!

Freedom from the shackles and lies of sin is *the* unique life changing experience the Gospel offers. It is truly the Good news! When we cut ourselves off from God –the source of all human dignity—we deprive ourselves of any real possibility of the true freedom to love, of loving even ourselves. Man was created for love to love. Yet, the principal results of sin are pride, fear of not being loved, and low self-worth, all of which are deeply rooted in us. Accepting our broken selves is much more difficult than it seems. Only the experience of one who loves us in a different way, unconditionally -- one who is capable of loving us without judging us and accepting us for who we are -- only this love has the power of moving us and changing our hearts. This is the particular grace of true reconciliation with God *because we are reconciled also with ourselves.* It is an experience of mercy. God the Father looks upon us and says "you are precious in my eyes, and honored, and I love you." (Isaiah 43:4) We can hear too the echo of the words of the Father in the parable of the prodigal son: 'you are with me always and all I have is yours" (Luke 15, 31). When we feel ourselves loved, despite our failings and our ugliness, then true freedom is experienced because love is the precondition to happiness and because freedom gives value to love. Truly, the law of Christianity is the law of freedom. It is the new law that Christ gives us: "Speak and act as those who are going to be judged by the law that gives freedom" (James 2, 12). Is not this the message the world so desperately needs to hear? You were created to love, to freely love, but you cannot try to win it for yourself as it is a gift from above. Christ's mercy opens each of us up to this free gift.

The Church offers the mercy of God when we are reconciled with Him and encounter this profound freedom from sin. Truly, this is the place where the Kingdom is first established, where every human heart tastes true freedom and true love. This Kingdom is Christ himself, when he is known, loved and imitated by every person. It is his Gospel of love when it becomes the rule of life in every heart. The motto of Regnum Christi --*Thy Kingdom Come*-- uttered with enthusiasm, and with such urgency among its members, above all expresses this desire to make it a reality in the world. To every man and woman seeking freedom in Christ in this world we say, "Thy Kingdom Come!" and echo the words of St Paul: "It is for freedom that

Christ has set us free. Stand firm, then, and do not let yourselves be burdened again by a yoke of slavery" (Galatians 5:1).

Questions for Group Discussion:

1. How am I bringing others to Christ's Kingdom? In what ways do I demonstrate authentic and generous charity?

2. What does it actually look like to "make myself a gift"? How do I avoid using others? Where are my greatest challenges in this regard?

3. Do I truly accept and love myself as Jesus does? How does this healthy self-regard allow me to love others? How does love of self and others set me free?

Chapter IV

Opposing the "kingdom of whatever"

We have not received the spirit of the world but the Spirit that is from God, so that we may understand the things freely given us by God.   *(I Corinthians: 2, 12)*

The "kingdom of whatever"[1] is a world of extreme pluralism, where meaning is self-invented by millions, and, therefore, society, as a whole, starves for meaning. Human experience shows us that *true meaning* is found in relationships. The dearth of real meaning in life is brought about by the dearth of relationships. There is no person living today in our current secular world who would not agree that our most important relationships are under serious strain, perhaps even under attack. Our most cherished memories in life are those when we are with others sharing experiences, and, yet, we seem to have less and less time for such relationships. We spend more time "busy" with material realities, in front of screens or playing with our phones than we do with more human realities like interacting with one another. In the "kingdom of whatever" human relationships are secondary--not to mention a relationship with God—and, this creates an existential emptiness in the human heart. "What few people seem to ponder is the fact that our emptiness hurts. We ache because we are not full. This is precisely the reason that every adult either is in hot pursuit of the ONE or is frantically seeking the many. Either we have God who does fill, or we are endlessly pursuing things which do not. It is because they do not fill that we endlessly pursue them."[2]

Regnum Christi aspires to build a Kingdom in this world that is not a nebulous cloud of "whatever" but flows from and is rooted in a relationship, even better, a friendship. This Kingdom begins always in relationship because God is a relationship, a relationship of persons. In fact, historically the word *person* came upon the language scene right when the early Christians were trying to figure out how to define God; and, more importantly, God as a relationship. It was a perfect fit to explain that God is in Himself a relationship of persons, *a loving communion of persons*: Father, Son and Holy Spirit. The book of Genesis seems to insinuate this communion of divine persons when we read the plural reference in Genesis 1:26: "Then God said: *Let us* make human beings in our image, after *our* likeness." Being made in the image of God, the human individual possesses the dignity of a person, who is not just something, *but someone*. He is capable of self-knowledge, of self-possession and of freely giving himself and entering into communion with other persons.[3] So like God, the human person is "relational" and was created out of love for love by God, called into existence for relationship with other persons.

Human relationships are a natural and necessary preparation for entering into relationship with God. So it follows, for example, that my relationship with my earthly father has much to do with how I relate to my heavenly father. If in human interaction, people of noble, kind and generous dispositions can so uplift and inspire others, how much more potent would be the effect of God on we his creatures. Yet, we need to pause on this point and reflect on just exactly what we are saying. The ancient Greeks used to ask: can a human being have a relationship with a divine person and their answer was a solemn IMPOSSIBLE! Human persons and God cannot have a relationship because they are too different; their lives are too far apart. But what if God became a *human person*? "How dramatically have the actions of the God-man Jesus Christ changed the human condition! Now, and only now, can a human person really have relationship with God, because He, first of all unilaterally, has shared His life with us. How wonderfully Jesus expresses this very point when he says that "no longer do I call you servants...but I call you friends" (John 15,15). We might say that He invited us into a divine conversation. From the limited perspective of natural reason, from the noble Aristotle's perspective, this is beyond the dreams of man. We must never take a relationship with God for granted, as though it could have been expected."[4]

At the same time, the whole purpose of our creation, the whole purpose of our redemption is so that we may be fully united with God in every aspect of our being. We [human beings] exist for union; we were created for union; we were redeemed for eternal union.[5] And it is Christ - God made man- who is the door to communion with this divine family. As the Church puts it "two natures, without any confusion whatsoever, but also without any possible separation, are the divine and the human."[6] Remember what we profess in the Christian faith: God became man so that man could become God. [7] Yes, however mind-blowing this sounds, we are touching on the *unmerited* consequence of being made in the image and likeness of God. We literally *live* in as much as we commune with Christ, the God-man, and then consequentially with one another; and, we are literally emptied and *die* if we do not. If we do not experience relationships of love, we suffer greatly.

31

Such is the harsh reality of living immersed in the "kingdom of whatever!"

For the Church, the first and fundamental path is the human person. Regnum Christi is passionately committed to the "same concern and desires to serve the whole person and every person, giving them Christ, who alone is man's savior in all of the dimensions and realities of his being. The movement begins with this need deeply rooted in the heart of each individual —the need for a personal encounter with Christ. Christ alone is the definitive and complete answer to man's most dearly held desires and aspirations, his thirst for transcendence, and his insatiable hunger for happiness. And yet knowing that love is the key to people's innermost lives, Regnum Christi proposes that the encounter with Christ begins here. While it is true that we cannot love what we do not know, in the arena of interpersonal relationships, we need to love a person if we are to get to know him deeply. Only through love can a believer enter into the depths of Christ's Heart and detect his deepest feelings, his liveliest desires and the intensity of his love."[8] Christ reveals man to himself and makes his supreme vocation clear,[9] a vocation to make oneself a gift to another. "The human person was not created to live in solitude. Love is mankind's essential calling or vocation. Only in love, that is to say in the gift of himself, can man discover the truth of his own being."[10]

The capacity we have as human beings to relate to one another cannot be taken for granted because ultimately our relationships give our lives true value. Our relational capacity flows from the very essence and identity of God our Creator, who is in Himself a loving communion of persons, and more specifically through Christ, the God-man, who is the living human image of that divine love. To respond to the emptiness of the *kingdom of whatever*, the mission of Regnum Christi is to bring as many people as possible into a relationship with Christ the King, founder of the true Kingdom. "The Movement presents the person of Christ as the supreme model, standard and inspiration for their Christian life to the men and women who approach its spirituality. It exhorts them to know him, love him, follow him and make him known to others. Intimate friendship with Christ is the door which again gives us access to the exchange of love for which we have been created."[11]

Questions for Group Discussion:

1. How strong are my relationships with others? How about my relationship with God? What other things am I pursuing that cannot fulfill me; that cannot fill me?

2. How committed am I to giving Christ to others? What keeps me from surrendering to what should be an uncontrollable urge to give others to Christ?

3. What do I see as my primary and ultimate vocation? What am I doing to keep my priorities straight?

Chapter V

Building the Kingdom of Christ through Communion

"I have often repeated the call for a new evangelization during these years. I repeat it again in order to emphasize that we must renew that original impulse and allow ourselves to be filled with the zeal of the apostolic preaching after Pentecost. We must awaken in ourselves those sentiments of St. Paul who exclaimed: "Woe to me if I do not proclaim the Gospel!" (St. John Paul II, *Novo millennio ineunte, n. 40*)

"To build the Kingdom of Christ" is to pass from, but never to leave, the encounter with Christ's mercy, an experience that brings deep gratitude and a new founded spirit of freedom, to the supernatural ambition of joining with Christ in the salvation and sanctification of the world. It is a call to respond freely in love to LOVE, to a love that was freely given. Yet, this change of heart is not something that happens overnight. "It is no accident that these new ecclesial realities like Regnum Christi include many converts, people who "come from afar." At the beginning of this conversion process there is always a personal encounter with Christ which radically transforms life; an encounter made possible by credible witnesses who re-live in the movement that unique experience of the first disciples: "come and see"

(John 1:46)."[1] These credible witnesses provide important relationships which sustain and build up this change of heart. It's like Christ inviting James and John to see where he lives, and, from that intimate time together, from that deeper communion, comes the response of the heart to want to go and share it as Andrew did with Simon Peter (cf. John 1, 39). Such human interaction with other committed followers of Christ show that this calling of Christ can in fact be lived out, that *you can do this*, you do not have to return to your former ways of living.   It is easy to imagine that St. Paul was getting at this as well when we hear him say: "Be imitators of me".

The Christian life must be "incarnational," it must be incarnated in persons. Then, and only then, does it become believable, moreover, it becomes "live-able." Literally, we believe it when we see it. Such a conversion process comes through relationships, through communion with others who are trying to live the same spirit. The Regnum Christi handbook states it so: "Ordinarily, you do not live your calling in Regnum Christi in isolation. The Movement is above all a true, spiritual family in the Church. Therefore, the life of its members unfolds in the framework of spiritual communion and fraternal charity, as always happened in the Church since early Christianity.

The good news of Christ *spread with contagious hope and joy from person to person*, wife to husband, parents to children, slave to master, and from these masters to their friends and acquaintances. Converting to the faith meant sharing it, beginning with your own family. Every Christian was an apostle; *every Christian community a living flame of the Church.* For the power of love cannot be contained."[2] One could say that the specific calling and mission of any Regnum Christi members consists in assimilating the reality and dynamism of this love which is both sublime and concrete: sublime with regard to how God mysteriously acts in our life through interior inspirations and human circumstances and concrete in the love of neighbor.

Regnum Christi is an *apostolic* movement. Words alone are not enough to make Christ's love known. It requires the witness of a life that is consistent with the demands of love. And love demands works.[3] Regnum Christi is convinced of the power of personal witness: the Movement encourages its members to show initiative and reminds them of their responsibility, rooted in baptism, to make faith the driving force of their daily lives in their personal, family, parish, professional and social environments.   Members of this spiritual family are not bystanders looking on, but to strive to inject into events the power and dynamism that are proper to Christianity. Just as faith without works is dead, so also love without works is locked in a pipedream.

Our mission crystallizes when each one of our members makes God's love known to others in any life situation whatsoever, and in any sector of society. Where this is going on the mission of the Movement is being carried out.[4] This is what we call the attitude of an apostle or an apostle of the Kingdom. Whether it be educating your children at home in this same spirit, through some specific apostolate in your parish, or at some event sponsored by Regnum Christi, such experiences bring incredible vitality to the conversion process of the heart. To witness in another person what you yourself have experienced is one of the most radical confirmations of the power of the Holy Spirit that one can experience in the apostolate. It breeds deeper convictions, zeal for the salvation of others, and new confidence. One of the great prophetic moments of the pontificate of St. John Paul II was his deep conviction that the ecclesial movements were a manifestation of a "new missionary advent," a great "Christian springtime," prepared by God. The Church faces the permanent challenge of effectively passing on the Gospel to each new generation. Christ needs arms! Christ needs feet!

Christ needs tongues! The apostles of the Kingdom of Christ must offer their very selves unconditionally so as to work for the interests of Christ and his Church!

Building the Kingdom is beyond urgent. Our modern world today with its stress on individualism is in dire need of leadership. We are desperate for a response to the plight of a culture lost in the values contrary to the Gospel. Common to all the members of the Regnum Christi family is our annual renewal retreat called the Spiritual Exercises based on the classical Ignatian model retreat first developed by St Ignatius of Loyola. The challenge of a truly Christian leadership is the underlying theme of a meditation in the Spiritual Exercises of St. Ignatius titled, *the Call of an Earthly King*. Its focus is on an earthly monarch who calls his people to follow him in his desire "to conquer all the lands of the infidel." He invites his good subjects to join him in this noble enterprise. The lesson for us in the 21st century is simple: strong leadership is the answer. Being a good Christian is not enough, the movement desires to form apostolic leaders committed to the never-completed task of evangelization. "Missionary outreach helps baptized persons discover the fullness of their own vocation; it helps them overcome the temptation of egoistic selfishness and the subtle danger of seeing the movement or community as a refuge or a way to flee the problems of the world in an environment of warm friendship."[5]

Building the Kingdom demands deep faith combined with a strong sense of mission and zeal to work tirelessly to combat the breakdown of Christian civilization, beginning with your own family and community. "These new charisms generate groups of people—men and women, youth and adults—who are solid in their faith, full of zeal, and ready to preach the Gospel. Here we are not talking about theoretical concepts, but rather "living" projects experienced in the concrete, personal lives of individuals and in the life of so many Christian communities. These are projects ready to happen…this is the great richness of the Church in our day."[6] To be "living projects" are exactly what the members of the Movement aspire to, "living signs" to the world that indicate the true path to personal and human fulfillment. To build and extend the Kingdom Christ through communion is to embrace the call of a lifelong project of conversion. It is allowing the Spirit of Christ to take over your heart, sharing this experience with others as God leads you, making an investment in your personal Christian formation to help sustain, develop and grow. May your Kingdom Come! It is never a done deal.

Questions for Group Discussion:

1. How is my response to Christ's love? Do I see it as a personal response, as it would be with my spouse, children, or friends?

2. What loving relationships have been inspirational to me? How have these inspirations affected my own relationships with my family?

3. How committed am I to being a lifelong project of conversion? How would others grade me as a living sign of God's true path to fulfillment? What areas of my life are in need of improvement in this regard?

Chapter VI

Core to the Kingdom:
Militia Christi

"Therefore, my beloved, as you have always obeyed, so now, not only in my presence but much more in my absence, work out your salvation with fear and trembling; for God is at work in you, both to will and to work for his good pleasure."
(Phil. 2: 12-13)

There are all kinds of descriptions about what's wrong with our current world, but there is one particular phrase that really seems to go to the heart of it: *existential boredom.* One writer sums it well: "When a person is existentially bored he may experience occasional pleasures, but for the most part his life is dreary, uninteresting, and loveless. To him it all appears useless. Though he may retain some capacity for sense pleasure, he is incapable of the thrill of joy. He does not respond to reality. Splendid scenery, beautiful music, intellectual keenness, a sparkling personality all leave him untouched and unmoved. He may know the dictionary definition of genuine love, but he has no experience of it. He is a stranger to enthusiasm, and he feels both rootless and restless. Because he is incapable of interpersonal depth, he is in love with no one. People in love are not bored. Nor are they in doubt about the beloved one."[1]

Doesn't it always come down to love? Genuine love is at stake. St John Paul II knew well the world's desperate need for Christ, for radical love, when he wrote: "Man cannot live without love. He remains a being that is incomprehensible for himself, his life is senseless, if love is not revealed to him, if he does not encounter love, if he does not experience it and make it his own, if he does not participate intimately in it".[2] Our world has lost its capacity to give and receive genuine love and hungers for people who love radically. The core of the Regnum Christi charism is Militia Christi[3] which in the end is about the way we aspire to love Jesus Christ. As one Legionary priest commented, *"Militancy is an attitude of the heart before Christ our Lord by which we are always ready to do His Will. The way we are militant is in the way we love ...we try to keep our spirit prompt, ready to act on the inspirations of the Holy Spirit, seeking to love more, to give ourselves to Christ evermore, and to give more to others."*[4]

What was clear to Pope Benedict, [5]and others before him, was that the Legion of Christ and the Regnum Christi Movement were combative in the way we try to live our Christian vocation, and he personally called us not to lose, but to preserve, our true nucleus, that of the *militia Christi,* which characterizes the apostolic and missionary action of the Church. Pope Paul VI also addressed the Legionaries in Rome in a 1974 General Audience on the same subject saying: "You are Legionaries, that is, not sedentary people or just lookers–on, but men who give shape to reality with your vigor, and give Christianity an expression that is distinctive to it: militancy. Legionary, that means you do battle in the name of Jesus. May God bless you and always preserve this characteristic quality".

We are desperate to recover and enkindle this kind of loving in the Christian world. Our Savior Jesus Christ shared the same sentiments in his heart: "I have come to bring fire on the earth, and how I wish it were already *kindled*" (Luke 12:48-50). The Regnum Christi Movement wants to respond to these sentiments in the heart of Christ. We base our Movement on unconditional love and self-surrender. This is the granite rock, this solid foundation, and we build all our apostolate upon it. To achieve this, we must not only look to do good on our own, but, with God's help, kindle in others the burning desire to do good. This will create a chain of evangelization and apostolate that will cross all boundaries. *If we can love like this, then we will move others to do the same. This was the way of the first Christians.* St. Paul called the Corinthians to *excel* in this love: "But since you excel in everything—in faith, in speech, in knowledge, in complete earnestness and in the love we have *kindled* in you—see that you also excel in this grace of giving" (2 Corinthians 8:6-8).

In other words, true love for Christ needs this expression. Genuine love is by its very nature extravagant and goes beyond what is asked: "If anyone presses you to go one mile, go with them two miles."(Matthew 5:40-42) The call to Regnum Christi is a vocation to love, but, more specifically, *to battle for love.* Here we find the fundamental difference between spiritual militancy and earthly militancy. As Pope Benedict observed it is not by power, force or violence that Christ's kingdom is extended, but with the *gift of self.* We must take love to the extreme, even toward our enemies. Jesus does not conquer the world with the strength of armies. He conquers them with the strength of the Cross! That is victory's true guarantee.[6] Those who fight to heed the law of love will live in peace. "If you pay attention to these laws and are careful to follow them, then the Lord your God will keep his covenant of love with you, as he swore to your ancestors" (Deuteronomy 7, 12). In contrast, in the world, without communication with God (prayer) we may "soldier on", even with very worthwhile goals, and even achieve great worldly success and power, but will we find peace? The prophet Isaiah called out the detractors of Israel on this point, those who looked on faith realities with disdain, by saying "Israel's watchmen are blind, they all lack knowledge; they are all mute dogs, they cannot bark; they lie around and dream" (Isaiah 56, 10).

We are called to be fighters because what is at stake is to lose genuine love, to allow its purity to be distorted by evil. Benedict XVI says that the members of the Church on earth are aptly described as *ecclesia militans*, i.e., the Church militant, since it is necessary for it to enter into battle with evil.[7] We want to defend our beloved from evil and so we fight. Of course the spirit of the Legionaries of Christ expresses the same. By its combative spirit, the religious of the community aspire to devote themselves with great love and zeal to the task of extending Christ's Kingdom in society and transmitting the light of the Gospel to the consciences of all people. They should see themselves as messengers of God's mystery, overcoming fatigue, difficulties and limitations of time, and energetically reject laziness and cowardice. When we think of a spirit of fight, we think of things like being attentive, vigilant, persevering, and courageous, a spirit of readiness to respond, rather than being stifled, discouraged, complaining, or even worse, bored! This call to

Regnum Christi is a call to reject existential boredom and embrace Divine Love!

When we think *militia Christi,* we do not think about being asleep. Yet, it is precisely *this* that is most glaringly obvious to us in the Church today: many, many are *asleep in the light.* Even the Church's leadership sees this clearly: "The 'calm conservation' vision of the Church which is so prevalent in certain circles today comes under direct challenge by the movements' vision of a missionary Church courageously projected toward new frontiers. This latter vision ought to help diocesan and parish pastoral programs recover a much needed prophetic, militant element. The Movements know how to draw out the spiritual potential of the laity by helping them smash the barriers of timidity, fear, and false complexes of inferiority which today's secular culture creates in the hearts of so many Christians. The movements' radical Christian 'way of being' is an indictment of that 'tired Christianity' (Benedict XVI) of so many baptized persons, that superficial Christianity rife with confusion."[8]

Yet, it is just too easy to be bitingly critical today of current events, of the Church's leadership, or even worse, to live with the attitude of "we have all the answers to the problems, the rest of you are useless." However, this cannot be the spiritual militancy of Regnum Christi. No ecclesial movement, or work of God, can allow the gift to become corrupted with pride. The personal history of the Legion and Regnum Christi shows this. These times challenge us to love radically, to respond with a spirit of responsibility, and, more importantly, a spirit of humility to the gift that God has given us. "The ecclesial movements and new communities are a truly 'providential gift' of God to the Church, a gift that should be received with a living sense of gratitude and responsibility so that the opportunity they represent is not squandered. This gift is both a task and a challenge for the lay faithful and the Church's Pastors".[9]

What task and what challenge? St. John Paul II never tired of insisting that the ecclesial movements and new communities are called to take their place "humbly in dioceses and parishes, serving the Church with an attitude wholly devoid of pride or superiority with regard to other realities and with a true spirit of sincere collaboration and ecclesial communion."[10] Regnum Christi's mission is not born of a passing need, nor is it based on currently fashionable ideas, but on the Church's urgent concern to make Christ's love known to mankind —for love is ultimately the essence of Christianity. And love is at one and the same time a joyful announcement and a binding commandment, reality and hope, a gift from God and a human task.[11]

Questions for Group Discussion:

1. Do I find myself bored with life? Is something holding me back from loving fully? How deeply am I able to love?

2. How militant am I in the way I love? How can I rekindle this kind of love in the Christian world?

3. Who of my brothers are "asleep in the light"? How is the Holy Spirit prompting me to help smash this timidity both responsibly and humbly?

Chapter VII

Forging an Apostle of the Kingdom in Solitude

"I delight to do your will, O my God; your law is within my heart." (Psalm 40:8)

There has never been a period in which such material wealth and advantage has been at the disposal of such a wide number as the present age. And yet not since Christianity began has the dissatisfaction been so profound and universal. Often times, so dominated by the material in this world, we neglect the spiritual and so suffer a profound void. The nature of the human person is such that it unites the spiritual and material worlds;[1] the person is an integrated whole of body and spirit; and, both need feeding to sustain the whole in happiness. To a world dominated by the material, if you cannot see it and touch it then it does not exist, it does merit serious attention. The spiritual world for most is simply a foreign concept. The contaminated air we breathe is so riddled with a material flavor-- literally at all levels-- that even the most upright of persons simply forget just how important the spiritual is. Hence, what follows is a sort of deep insecurity; and, so often, we are not quite sure what is wrong with us, "…maybe we need another vacation, or a trip to the spa," so many say to themselves. Like the blinking light on the dashboard of our car, with the oil running low, so too our spirits tell us with fatigue, impatience, confusion, and even despair that something has to change! Behold the experience of most people on the planet, even baptized Christians, living in the 21st century.[2]

The mission of Regnum Christi is to call us back to our beginnings, to the remembering of who we are and why we call ourselves followers of Christ. This process is called forging the "new man;" and, it is just that: a process. It takes time and effort like anything worthwhile. "The baptized person is already a new man but he has before him the task of cooperating with God's grace to attain "the stature of the perfect man, the maturity of Christ's fullness" (Eph 4:13). This cooperation begins with *interior renewal* that is the fruit of divine grace."[3] We do not need more of the "external," but rather more of the internal. The answer to the "empty tank" syndrome described above is first found in something that St. John Paul II called *Original Solitude*.[4] In the Pope's teaching, it was like he was telling us to go back to Genesis when the first human being (Adam) was alone with God and find out what he learned and do the same. Observe how your relationships will get better and the void will be filled. Almost like a direct answer to the question of how to recover true meaning in life the Pope says: Man "must rediscover the lost fullness of his humanity and want to regain it."[5] Do I want to break free from the extremes of our materialistic world where "having" overrides the importance of "being?" Do I want to reclaim what makes me fully human? Then begin with solitude.

Assuming the answer is, "yes," then the first lesson in forging the new man is to ***stop***. Stop the activity. We need solitude. And we need not be afraid of silence or of God. Remember that God is the source of all relationship, moreover the source of all meaning in life. Adam was alone with God and "finds himself from the first moment of his existence before God in search of his own being… in search of his own 'identity'."[6] Solitude is the door to true communion. Solitude will give us answers to the most important questions of our human existence and identity. And, if we already know those answers, then it will only confirm them and make those convictions stronger -- answers like God is God, and I am not. It is an interior journey. "Man is called to this rediscovery by the word of the Gospel....if he allows them to work in him he can at the same time hear in his innermost being the echo, as it were, of that 'beginning,' of that good 'beginning' to which Christ appealed on another occasion to remind his listeners who man is, who woman is, and who they are reciprocally one for the other in the work of creation".[7] Even with sin, if we have failed God and feel ashamed of our failings, "we still experience a certain 'echo' of the original innocence of Man".[8] God does not want us to forget him and the peace He alone can give; "peace I leave with you; my peace I give you. I do not give to you as the world gives" (John 14:27). Solitude is not sitting there in the dark somewhere in your house waiting for something to happen, rather it is a door to listening to the echo of *the Other* --with or without words-- and brings meaning because it brings us into a relationship with a personal God, who speaks to us in the echo of our longings for Him. Dramatic things can happen with just a little bit of solitude with the Lord. The best examples of this in the Gospel is the Samaritan women at the well who, seemingly so far from God, having been married five times, encounters Christ, and, after her conversation with him, exclaims, *"He told me everything I ever did!"* (John 4:39)

When exposed to more solitude, the first apparent change that happens to us is that we want more of it. The more we are exposed to the climate where God speaks, the more we desire to feel the warmth of His light. It's like you have awakened from a slumber and you see things in a different way: "Wake up sleeper, rise from the dead, and

Christ will shine on you." St. Paul continues, "for you were once darkness, but now you are light in the Lord....find out what pleases the Lord. Have nothing to do with the fruitless deeds of darkness, but rather expose them" (Ephesians 5:8-9). It is like a switch goes off; and, we begin to worry about our spiritual life and what really is important in life. "Contact with God through prayer is a source of certainties and convictions, attitudes and particular behavior. The praying person senses the need to adapt his mind, heart, will and activity to the most holy will of God who has come to meet him, 'Lord, what do you want me to do?" [9]

Perhaps, for the first time ever, we begin to understand what the word *conversion* means. In order to forge the new man in Christ, the Christian must work to strip himself of the old man, with his disordered inclinations of sensuality, vanity and pride, and to appropriate for himself the new heart that God has given him in baptism, by means of his communion with Christ and the Church. In this way, by the action of the Holy Spirit, he gradually acquires a heart that is open to his Creator and the vocation God has given him; a pure heart, inscribed with God's law, the law of love; a meek and humble heart, like Christ's. [10] The forging begins with solitude.

Solitude with God also brings with it deep meaningful communion with other persons, especially if they have Christ at the center of their lives. Anyone that prays will tell you this. We begin to seek out those who we instinctually sense are "in the light" and this can create some very unique bonds with other people who share Christ. "They were of one heart and one mind" (Acts 4:32). So it was with the early Church. "Impelled by the love instilled in their hearts, the first Christians would gather in small communities to pray and to receive the teachings of the Apostles, forming a single body in Christ. In their turn the Apostles and their successors began setting up local churches through which the Kingdom of God became increasingly present in the world. Christianity was like the yeast of which Christ spoke, and little by little it transformed society, it spread out among families, acquaintances and fellow workers."[11]

However, with the joys come the sorrows, as close "friends" begin not liking this more spiritual side of you. They are not bad people, but they do not seem to see what you now see and are maybe caught up in the shadows of the world. Sadly, our world is filled with the profile of such people. The prophet Isaiah has some striking words to describe what goes on with them, "So justice is far from us, and righteousness does not reach us. We look for light, but all is darkness; for brightness, but we walk in deep shadow" (Isaiah 59:9). Such tribulations bring you to seek more solitude, and, hence, more prayer. "Prayer is also a condition for the apostolate. According to the principle of the primacy of grace, God is the only source of fruitfulness and effectiveness in the supernatural order.

The Christian will be an instrument of salvation for his brothers and sisters only to the degree that he is united with Christ, "for without me you can do nothing" (John15:5). So, often it is prayer alone that is able to open hearts to Christ's love, give grace its victory over sin and get people to accept the demands of the Kingdom."[12] With the help of divine grace, this forging demands a continual conversion in solitude, since in this life the Christian has not yet crossed the finish line. The road after our initial conversion is still one that requires our effort to clothe ourselves with the new man. It is not without its great joys and lights from the Lord, but it also has its dark valleys in which we must persevere with trust, relying on the goodness of the Lord who died and rose again.

Questions for Group Discussion:

1. How have I allowed the material world to deter me from the spiritual life? Where do I experience voids in my life?

2. What positive steps am I taking to forge the "new man"? When do I schedule solitude in my life to be in communion with God? Am I seeking more?

3. How do I connect with like-minded spiritual friends? How have tribulations increased my prayer life? How am I becoming an instrument of salvation?

Chapter VIII

The Kingdom makes all things new.

"If you are in Christ, you are a new creation…"

(2 Cor. 5:17)

The principal enemy of our new life in Christ is our egotism – and it affects the very identity of every man and women, marriage, family, community. Due to human weakness and the depravity of our culture, we can question whether such a transformation or real change of heart in the human person is even possible. "In keeping with the Church's thoroughly realistic and wise understanding of human nature, Regnum Christi recognizes in man a mystery of greatness and misery, holiness and sinfulness, strength and weakness. It leans neither to fatalistic pessimism nor naïve optimism. It wishes to offer this human person, often burdened with deep internal contradictions, a path of constant improvement, one full of hope in spite of man's stumbling and falls; for we are convinced that God's love is stronger than man's weakness."[1] If the human person is in fact a *new creation,* as St. Paul claimed before the first Christians in Corinth, what does this transformation in grace look like in a given man or woman, or even in a marriage? The following reflection hopes to offer some specific characteristics on how the Movement embarks on this project of forming the new man or woman in Christ.

Regnum Christi is open to all people, weak and in need of help, and invites them to enter the path that leads to salvation in Christ. As an ecclesial movement, it welcomes those who want to undertake the journey toward Christ and to distinguish themselves in following him. It is a narrow and demanding path where you often progress in small steps; and, it requires patience, courage and support to accept the reality and conditions of Christ's Kingdom. *Hope* is the first characteristic in constructing this new creation born in Christ through baptism, how could it be otherwise? The reality of our own brokenness and that of those around us can bring skepticism, much skepticism. Like St. Paul, we need to beg for the eyes to see this great hope we have *in Christ*, "May God our Father, enlighten the eyes of our hearts, so that we may see the great hope to which we are called in Christ Jesus"(Ephesians 1:18). Such skepticism can bring controversy too. For example, some of the teachings of St. John Paul II are controversial, particularly regarding the idea that the power of grace wrought by Christ can transform our desires and liberate our hearts from the domination of concupiscence, our fallen condition. He states: "Redemption is a truth, a reality, in the name of which man must feel himself called, and "called with effectiveness....man must feel himself called to rediscover, or even better, to realize ...the freedom of that spiritual state and power that derive from mastery over the concupiscence of the flesh." (cf. TOB 46, 4) Even though the heart in many respects has become a battlefield between genuine love and concupiscence (our fallen condition), the power to express genuine love by which man, through is masculinity and femininity becomes a gift for the other has in some measure continued to permeate and shape the love born in the heart." Do we distrust then the heart because of the battle, the Pope asks, No is his answer! It is only to say that we must remain in control of it [the heart].[2]

Yes, it is clear from the very beginning of human existence, the battle for the human heart was at stake: "The Lord saw how great the wickedness of the human race had become on the earth, and that every inclination of the thoughts of the human heart was only evil all the time"(Genesis 6:5). However, with the dawning of Christianity, the battle, and, more importantly, *the hope* for redemption in Christ was ever more apparent. True hope comes first in the recognition of a change of lifestyle through baptism which being *in Christ*, as St. Paul attests, means to: "remember that at that time you were separate from Christ, excluded from citizenship in Israel and foreigners to the covenants of the promise, without hope and without God in the world" (Ephesians 2:12). The hope of redeeming the whole of the human person—body, mind, and spirit—is also clear here in St. Paul writing to the Philippians, "I eagerly expect and hope that I will in no way be ashamed, but will have sufficient courage so that now as always Christ will be exalted in my body, whether by life or by death." (Philippians 1:20) Hope also comes in celebrating the fruits of the new man inspired by the example of others, "We remember before our God and Father your work produced by faith, your labor prompted by love, and your endurance inspired by hope in our Lord Jesus Christ" (1 Thessalonians 1:3).

The powerful witness of holy men and women who have gone before us shows us the inexhaustible possibilities that come from an openness to the life of grace. "There is a new interest in the study of the lives of the saints not based on some pious curiosity but rather a growing realization that the saints, and the saints alone, have found what other men and women are vainly seeking –real life!"[3] These men and women know their weakness, they know that they are truly vessels of clay, and any good that comes, come from the very power of God: "we are only vessels of clay that hold this treasure, to make it clear that such overwhelming power comes from God and not from us" (2 Cor 4:7). When we come in contact with their lives, they give us hope, the hope to stay the course, that this walk with Christ is truly worthwhile!

The second characteristic the Movement proposes is *realism*. We are all painfully aware just how often we let God down with our choices of selfishness over genuine love. Our hearts literally groan at their own waywardness. Redemption of the whole person in Christ --thoughts, desires, and feelings -- is an undertaking that is not for the faint of heart. It is an extremely taxing journey. St. Paul was no stranger to this and describes with acute accuracy, in his letter to the sensual Romans, the redemptive process, "We know that the whole creation has been groaning as in the pains of childbirth right up to the present time. Not only so, but we ourselves, who have the first fruits of the Spirit, groan inwardly as we wait eagerly for our adoption to sonship, the redemption of our bodies...for in this hope we were saved" (Romans 8, 22-23). The purification is real and necessary because the cost of our salvation was real and necessary. "You yourselves were once alienated from him; you nourished hostility in your hearts because of your evil deeds. But now Christ has achieved reconciliation for you in his mortal body by dying, so as to present you to God holy, free of reproach and blame" (Colossians 1:21-22). This realism is motivated by the hope we have. The Lord *does* hear our groaning and *remembers* his promises: "God heard their groaning and he remembered his covenant with Abraham, with Isaac and with Jacob" (Exodus 2:24).

Christian realism necessarily embraces the reality of *sacrifice*, a third characteristic. This means coming to grips with the cost of our redemption. Redemption was won for us through the cross; and, the cross for us human beings means one word: sacrifice. *To know Christ* and the sacrifice he made for us is the stepping stone to more realism. For the great Apostle St. Paul, this knowledge was imperative, "For I decided to know nothing among you except Jesus Christ, and him crucified"(1 Corinthians 2:2). In Regnum Christi, our conversion to Christ comes with first knowing him as our member handbook states, "Our first spiritual need is to know Christ more, to the point of attaining a deep experience of his person and his love. Therefore, it is not a knowledge based exclusively on academic study, but rather an interior knowledge, that comes from prayer, faith and love. It is knowledge based on experience more than theory, knowing more with our heart than our mind. It is not a feeling –though it doesn't exclude feelings and is grateful for those that are helpful– but the gift of self. [4] We must reach the point where we are imitating Him interiorly with our own decision, to turn our will over to him, to be aligned with his will. The optimal places to receive this experience of Christ are prayer, the sacraments and in particular the Eucharist, the Gospel, and the contemplation of the mysteries of Christ's life, especially his Incarnation, Passion, Death and Resurrection. To begin "knowing Christ" is to begin imitating Christ, however difficult. "To live the ideal of charity maturely, we must bear the inevitable burdens and even tensions that daily living gives rise to, especially when the tasks we have to do together with others are difficult and subject to human error and failure. No one ought to nourish the false hope of living an imaginary, disembodied charity. Loving is giving. And so this virtue is practiced and forged every day, in every instant. You are a Christian by loving here and now." [5]

Contained in Christ's invitation to his followers (but often missed) is actually a four stage process to check your realism in the daily following of the Lord through sacrifice. We can break this invitation up into four parts: (1) "if anyone wishes, (2) he must deny himself, (3) take up his cross, and (4) follow me." (Luke 23, 9) The first part is "if anyone wishes". The *Latin* for "wish," *volere,* can also be translated to want or will. A person's wants often lead to one's desires or moods at a given moment, to what is in the heart. We need not be afraid for Christ knows our hearts and he proves this time and time again in the Gospel, "Immediately Jesus knew in his spirit what they were thinking in their hearts, and he said to them, 'why are you thinking these things?'" (Mark 2:8) The new man stands or falls by what is in his heart, so inviting Christ into our world to help us untangle our disordered desires is a critical first step. Hence, self-knowledge is an essential part to this spirit of realism.

The second stage of Christ's invitation is to "deny yourself." Your desires will not always want to "behave" themselves; they will not always want to follow what the "head" is telling them is true. And so you will need to say "no" to them. Plato used to reckon the disordered desires of our hearts as to a train of horses that need guidance by way of reason. We educate our hearts through the practice of self-control out of love and can do so in variety of ways: faithfully and carefully fulfilling our duties; developing a stronger mastering over all the fickleness of our feelings and emotions; tempering our character; controlling our disordered emotional reactions; and, finally, renouncing anything that might hinder our giving ourselves to God and to others.

The third stage of the invitation is to "pick up your cross." Your cross is not my cross. We all have very specific crosses to bear each day that God has allowed. What am I doing with these crosses? Running from them, denying them, or complaining about them? The late Bishop Fulton Sheen used to say that there is so much wasted suffering in the world. Am I wasting my suffering on complaining, on the "blame game", on not embracing with love, what God sends me for my sanctification? Christ is calling me to suffer with him. Finally, the fourth stage is to "Come follow me." The four stages actually build on each other. Only when we really desire to follow Christ with our hearts and consciously choose Him (stage 1), will we then begin the journey of self-denial (stage 2) and embrace our daily crosses (stage 3). Only when we live the first three stages, can we really say "I follow Christ" (stage 4).

These stages of spiritual maturity, of knowledge and of love are often called the journey of the interior life. It's a journey that we make *with Christ. Everything we do* should be done *with Christ*; our Lord, master, and friend. "Christ-centeredness is the primary and specific characteristic of the Movement's spirituality and we are called to strive with all our strength to put on Christ in our hearts and in our actions, embracing the cross and self-denial out of love for the Lord, so that *Christ's life will be manifest in our life*.[6] To attain the really good things in life always takes sacrifice, often the restraint of our more ugly side. Self-denial is a Christian virtue by which we renounce our egotism and everything that is a hindrance to our greater love for God and our neighbor. Christ did say, "those who lose their life for my sake will find it" (Mt 16:25). The more deeply I abandon myself to Christ, the more completely I let Him penetrate my being, the more powerfully He, the Creator, gains authority in me, the more I become myself."[7] Christ has come to redeem our hearts, to win them back, to heal and transform them into gold tested in fire. There is no better example of such gold tested in fire than St. Paul: "I regard everything as loss because of the surpassing value of knowing Christ Jesus my Lord. For his sake I have suffered the loss of all things, and I regard them as rubbish, in order that I may gain Christ" (Philippians 3:8).

The Regnum Christi proposes a fourth characteristic that is the virtue of *perseverance*. Many who embark on the journey of the interior life abandon ship when the storms come, either because of spiritual immaturity or because they do not have the support needed. The ongoing formation offered by Regnum Christ wants to help the Christian to eliminate those possibilities and make holiness of life accessible. St. Paul compares the Christian's life to training so as to win first place in the stadium. The birth of this new creation is both divine and human. It is initiated by God: "Do not be astonished that I said to you, you must be born from above" (cf. John 3) and comes forth like the purification of gold in the human person, demanding training and ongoing education. Through Catholic formation, involving personal spiritual guidance, a structured prayer regime helping one stay focused, the accountability of other members in team, and the fuel of giving yourself to your first apostolate (specific vocation in life) we begin buffing like a diamond that image of Christ impressed in our very spirits. Again, St. Paul is convinced of this: "Just as we have borne the image of the man of dust, we will also bear the image of the man of heaven" (1 Corinthians 15:49).

Questions for Group Discussion:

1. How do I battle my own egotism? In what ways do I take advantage of the path of spiritual improvement that either the Church and/or the Movement offers?

2. How do I allow Christ to enlighten my heart so that I can see and act from an intelligence informed by the heart? How would others see that I have been redeemed body, mind and spirit? What do I do when I feel like giving up?

3. Where am I on the journey of the spiritual life? What causes me to fall off this path?

Chapter IX

Center piece of the Kingdom: His Sacred Heart

Part and parcel of our devotion to the Sacred Heart of Jesus is also our ability to offer ourselves generously to spread Christ's love to everyone by word and deed, trying to be for others an image of Jesus' merciful face.

(Regnum Christi Member Handbook, no. 75)

The charism of the Regnum Christi Movement finds its inspiration in the Sacred Heart spirituality and has so since the foundations of the Legion of Christ in the 1940's. The first name of the community was in fact listed as the *Missionaries of the Sacred Heart and Mother of Sorrows.* The Legionaries were founded in very turbulent times in the history of Mexico, with a civil war ending in 1917, and religious persecutions reaching their height in the 1920's with the Cristero War. The people witnessed horrific violence against the Church and against its priests. The persecution continued into the 1930's, and beyond, with anti-Church governments. With such terrible sufferings came a deep spirituality in the people above all rooted in a devotion to the Sacred Heart of Jesus and to his Blessed Mother. One can imagine from such suffering how this new work of

God would first be named after the heart of Jesus and dedicated to his mother, especially under her title, "Mother of Sorrows." During this same time, Pope Pius XI established, in 1929, the universal feast of Christ the King in the Church, attempting to complete and bring to perfection the consecration of the world to the Sacred Heart of Christ, which had been made by Pope Leo XIII back in 1899. The two Popes saw the Kingdom of Christ and the Kingdom of the heart of Jesus as one in the same thing. Christ desires to reign through his heart and through his love. All of this history can guide us to the inspirational reason why the spiritual family of the Legion is called, in fact, *Regnum Christi*, *Latin* for "Kingdom of Christ."

Such deep piety intensified a real, evangelical missionary spirit in the country already present through "Popular Missions", a long-standing tradition of Catholic heritage in many predominately Catholic countries. These were essentially "forums" to preach the Gospel across the country to parish communities: bringing the people together to pray, to learn about their faith, and giving them hope. It was not that the persecutions produced this phenomena but surely intensified their vitality, especially through saintly witnesses like St. Rafael Guizar Valencia, Bishop of Vera Cruz, who was present at the beginnings of

the Legion, as well as a zealous apostle of Christ.
St. Rafael traveled all over his diocese leading
these popular missions. These popular missions
also allowed the Catholic community to support
and help one another under such difficult anti-
religious circumstances. One could draw a parallel
to the historical phenomena in the Church of the
new ecclesial movements, like Regnum Christi,
raised up by the Holy Spirit, helping people live
their faith in difficult secular circumstances. "Once
again the Spirit has intervened in the history of the
Church, raising up new charisms that possess an
extraordinary missionary dynamism which
responds in an opportune way to the challenges of
our time, great and dynamic as they
are." [1] Despite the obvious trials of being Catholic,
the first Legionaries often describe those years as
times of great spiritual vitality and hope, grounded
in a deep identification with the suffering heart of
Christ and united with an evangelical spirit to bring
people the Gospel of hope "to the ends of the
earth." Such historical circumstances afforded the
right soil to sow the first seeds of the Legion's
work and spirituality.

With such historical influence, Regnum
Christi instills in its members a Christ-centered
spirituality by way of a true devotion to the Sacred
Heart of Jesus, "which consists in the worship of

God's infinite and merciful love for all people expressed in Jesus Christ." [2] From the private revelations between our Lord Jesus and St. Margaret Mary Alacoque, which were to reveal to many Catholics the *infinite mercy* of the Sacred Heart of Christ, there are natural parallels in the Movement's spirituality and mission that are worth pondering. These parallels are not, of course, exclusive to a single spirituality, but rather can be found to exist in others as well. Yet, in the Regnum Christi Movement, the unique interplay between the priests of the Legion and the missionary zeal of our incorporated laity, including Consecrated Women and Men, single persons, married persons and youth, derives its origin from a charism which may be described *as a wellspring of mercy for sinners.*

Our priests and laity are called to be apostles of Christ's mercy in the Church and in the world, in a unique way which, over the course of our relatively brief history, has born the fruits of repentance and continuous conversion. In light of our recent history, it has become crystal clear that God's power and mercy shines forth by working through the weakest of instruments to bring about his work. It is due to this that we must continue to meditate on the three streams that flow from the Heart of Christ, as expressed in the Sacred Heart devotion. Thus meditating, we will see where we have been, who we are and where we are going, allowing the Holy Spirit to guide us.

First Stream

In 1673, commenting on the revelations of the Sacred Heart, St. Margaret Mary Alacoque speaks of *three streams that flow from the Heart of Christ.* "The first is the stream of mercy for sinners; it pours into their hearts sentiments of contrition and repentance."[3] Regnum Christi finds its mission in the preaching of the Kingdom, in extending the reign of Christ's heart, through grace, in each and every person. Christ announced the Kingdom with the words: "The Kingdom of God is at hand, repent and believe" (Mark 1:14). His Kingdom begins with repentance and mercy, with the turning away from sin, allowing for His salvific grace to pour into the hearts of sinners special graces of contrition and love. With the words "Go and sin no more," as priests, the Legionaries have witnessed the power of the sacrament of reconciliation; and, without really ever stating it, have allowed themselves to be apostles of God's mercy. From the earliest years of foundation, the Legionaries have had a particular devotional spirit --for lack of better words-- towards the power of encountering God's mercy in this sacrament. The seminarians of the community are imbued with this devotional spirit from the outset by the example of the priests. Without any hesitation, everyone knows that this encounter with mercy in confession is available on the hour 24/7. The members of Regnum Christi also know this first hand and live the sacrament with great delicacy, allowing for a more sensitive conscience which produces a more delicate love. Nothing is as important as to bring God's mercy to a soul, so that the soul can experience this freedom in Christ's love. As an apostle of mercy, a Legionary priest can identify with the words of the prophet Isaiah, as Christ did, making the same words his own, "The Spirit of the Lord is on me, because he has anointed me to proclaim good news to the poor. He has sent me to proclaim freedom for the prisoners and recovery of sight for the blind, to set the oppressed free" (Luke 4, 18).

Second Stream

St. Margaret Mary speaks of the second stream flowing from his Heart as "the stream of charity which helps all in need and especially aids those seeking perfection to find the means of surmounting their difficulties."[4] The Movement aspires to offer the human person, often burdened with deep internal contradictions, a path of constant improvement, one full of hope, in spite of man's stumbling and falls. For we are "convinced that God's love is stronger than man's weakness"[5] Many other ecclesial movements or associations, like Regnum Christi, are aiding people to find Christ and seek perfection on their journey in life. As the Pontifical Congregation for the Laity has said about the new movements, "Thanks to these charisms, many people have met Christ for the first time and believed in him or have returned to the Church and the sacraments after years of being away. So many people have gone from being Christians in name only to believers who are convinced and committed. How many fruits of authentic holiness of life! How many families that have been reconstituted in mutual love and fidelity! How many vocations to the priesthood, consecrated life, and new expressions of lay life according to the evangelical counsels!" [6]

How such fruits must console the heart of Christ! Truly, our ecclesial family is a *gift* to Mother Church, an outpouring of love and mercy through the ministerial priesthood of the Legionaries and the dedication of the lives of the laity in Regnum Christi. We are free to allow the storms of our foundation to draw us closer to the wounded side of our Savior. He loved us first, and, is, in time and eternity, willing to heal our every wound. Our member handbook exhorts us that only through "love can a believer enter into the depths of Christ's Heart and detect his deepest feelings, his liveliest desires and the intensity of his love, and live the truth that love is this: not that we have loved God but that he has loved us and sent his Son as expiation for our sins" [7]

Third Stream

From the third stream flows "love and light for the benefit of his friends who have attained perfection; these he wishes to unite to himself so that they may share his knowledge and commandments and in their individual ways, devote themselves wholly to advancing his glory"[8] As our member handbook states, "Part and parcel of our devotion to the Sacred Heart of Jesus is also our ability to offer ourselves generously to spread Christ's love to everyone by word and deed, trying to be for others an image of Jesus' merciful face." Looking to advance the cause of the Heart of Christ through the mobilization of new apostles is the singular conviction of the Legion and Regnum Christi. We aspire to dedicate our energies to educate a new generation of committed Catholics whose leadership will share this friendship with Christ and have the "indisputable ability to awaken the apostolic enthusiasm and missionary courage of the laity and will draw out the spiritual potential of the laity by helping them smash the barriers of timidity, fear, and false complexes of inferiority which today's secular culture creates in the hearts of so many Christians."[9]

Many of the Legionary priests and members of Regnum Christi have experienced just this: "deep inner transformation, at times to their own surprise; in fact, many never would have imagined themselves preaching the Gospel in this way or participating so actively in the Church's mission." [10] Such is the power of the encounter with the heart of Christ! *A true calling to Regnum Christi means, above all, a desire in one's very soul to study the Heart of Christ.* Through meditation and sharing with each other, we desire to assimilate in our own hearts what we see and experience in Christ's Heart, so full of love and mercy for sinners. To experience God's love, we must fix our eyes on the face of Christ, at once human and divine, suffering and transfigured, just and merciful. We must contemplate that Holy Face, which enlightens and strengthens the steps of all those who approach him.

From the Three Streams to Living the Virtues

This devotion to the Sacred Heart is also expressed through the exercise of two virtues: meekness and humility. Christ embodied these in an eminent way during his life, and he himself told his disciples to imitate him in them. The Church invites all to do the same with the words: *Jesus, meek and humble of heart, make my heart more like yours.* "How necessary for contemporary humanity is the message that flows from contemplation of the Heart of Christ. Where, indeed, if not from that source, will we be able to attain the reserves of meekness and forgiveness necessary to heal the bitter conflicts that bloody it? [11] *Humility* is the cornerstone of all the virtues and the virtue by which the human person accepts the truth about himself in his dealings with God, with others and with himself. It is the true spiritual poverty that leads you to recognize the reality of being a creature: you are radically dependent on God in your being and actions, you received everything from your Creator's love and, injured by sin, you are in need of mercy and redemption.[12] For the entire family of the Legionaries and Regnum Christi, the Sacred Heart devotion is summed up with the words of St. John Paul II:

In order to save man, victim of his own disobedience, God wished to give him a "new heart," faithful to his will of love (see Jeremiah 31:33; Ezekiel 36:26; Psalm 50[51]:12). This heart is the heart of Christ, the masterpiece of the Holy Spirit, which began to beat in the virginal womb of Mary and was pierced by the lance on the cross, thus becoming for all the inexhaustible source of eternal life. That Heart is now the pledge of hope for every man.[13]

Questions for Group Discussion:

1. How have I recognized God's merciful love in sending His Son? Have I allowed God's mercy to work through me?

2. How often do I take advantage of the sacrament of reconciliation? How do I respond to Christ's mercy for me by responding in charity to my brothers?

3. What am I really doing to spread Christ's love in word and deed? How humble am I in performing these works? Am I becoming an "Apostle of mercy"?

Chapter X

A Kingdom of Desire: Passionate love for Christ

I have loved you with an everlasting love (Jer 31, 3).

When one hears the word passion it is not normally in reference to God or the divine, rather it has typically more human, even sensual, connotations. When you think of passion, you think of desire, something deep in the self that needs expression, which even demands expression. When one speaks of a passionate love for God, such an idea is outside the "normal Joe's" human experience; in fact, it would probably be viewed as extreme. Today it is acceptable to be passionate about sports, politics, even pet animals, but not about God. The Regnum Christi Movement proposes a passionate love for Jesus Christ as the flame that lights the soul, a love that must come first and above all other loves. Passion is a word to describe the catalyzing effect that begins to happen when people meet Christ and let him into their life, most importantly, into their souls. Passion for something speaks of zeal, of serious commitment, of being "all in." By proposing this passionate love for Christ, it does not mean that you are an extremist, or even worse, that if your love for God is not passionate then "you are out," or some kind of second class Christian. Rather, it is a call to let God in, to open your very life to His loving Goodness and to let it be consumed like fire. "The holy power of God's love sears through us like a flame."[1]

Love for anything takes hold of us gradually as the knowing of the object of love grows. "You can't love what you don't know," as the saying goes. The member handbook says that "our experience of God's love in Christ necessarily tends to become something living. For a Christian, experiencing Christ deeply means living in love, living to love, and nourishing our life on love. Our life can now have no other motivation, meaning or goal than Christian love."[2] Passionate love means that you are consumed by a calling deep inside to love God and others the way Christ did. God is the source of all Good, all Truth, all Power and all that is Beautiful, and He merits our passionate love. St. Thomas Aquinas says that *the things that we love tell us what we are*. It makes sense to love the source of all Goodness, of all Truth, of all Beauty because this is what we long to be for ourselves and for others: true, and good and beautiful. "Human love is preordained to the Savior from the beginning, as its model and end almost like a casket so large and wide as to be able to receive God...the desire of the soul goes only to Christ. Here is the place of its rest, since he alone is the good, the truth and everything which inspires love." [3] Rewritten - Unconditional love for any created reality will not bring us the fulfillment for which we yearn. It is only a consuming love for God that will fulfill our deepest desires. I am good only in as much as God is good. You become what you love. In opposition to this, the culture encourages passionate "loves" for just about any created thing except for God who created the visible we so love.

Referencing passion with the subject of God is foreign to the ears of today because God does not like wild passion, right? God wants everybody to be well-behaved good little boys and girls. But let's challenge this: if we human beings are made in his image and likeness, and if passion is such a big part of the human experience, then there must be some form of passion in God himself who wired us this way. The most erotic book in the Old Testament, the Song of Songs, was written to reflect God's passionate love for his creatures: "You are all beautiful, my love, my dove, and there is no blemish in you" (Song 4, 7)...open to me my love, my dove, my perfect one" (Song 5, 2). *God is a passionate lover*. St. Gregory the Great speaks of this in his commentary on the Song of Songs: "Gods work with us; for he reaches down into the vocabulary of our sensual love in order to set our hearts on fire, aiming to incite us with holy loving...for from the words associated with this sensual love we learn how fiercely we are to burn with love for the Divine".[4]

Like St. Gregory, the saints show clearly that the Christian faith does not ignore or oppose the fact that our hearts have deep longings, that this is part and parcel of the primordial phenomena of human love. Christ came to redeem the entire human person and calls us to face in ourselves the unpurified elements of our fallen nature –so fractured by selfishness. These unpurified elements -as long as they remain unpurified- are ignoble and not worthy of our dignity as children of God. It is a calling to renounce the lies that such false and unworthy love spin in our hearts. This calling is a resounding YES to eros (passion) but to that eros with all its *original* and positive potential. Pope Benedict sums it up well: "An intoxicated and undisciplined *eros*, then, is not an ascent in "ecstasy" towards the Divine, but a fall, a degradation of man. Evidently, *eros* needs to be disciplined and purified if it is to provide not just fleeting pleasure, but a certain foretaste of the pinnacle of our existence, of that beatitude for which our whole being yearns."[5]

St. Thomas continues that the "love of a suitable good perfects and betters the lover; but love of a good which is unsuitable to the lover, wounds and worsens him. Wherefore man is perfected and bettered chiefly by the love of God: but is wounded and worsened by the love of sin".[6] We are called to be consumed with that which perfects us, which makes us better. Passionate love for Jesus Christ, true God and true man, the perfect man, makes me a better human being, a better lover. Salvation from sin always means the re-direction of our passion, from unsuitable loves to a worthy love. Divine love perfects human love. Hence the Church calls us to a life of *ascesis* which enhances the mastery of the will over its acts. Ascesis is another word for our constant and free collaboration with the action of grace in our life to restrain all the selfish and impure in the human heart in order to "maintain the integrity of the powers of life and love placed in us. This integrity ensures the unity of the person; it is opposed to any behavior that would impair it."[7]

For those who have undergone this journey know full well that there is no holiness of life without renunciation and spiritual battle. Human passion has a trajectory and it will end up wherever it is aimed! Give your passion proper aim, and it will bring you to the stars! Christ came to save us from that false trajectory by re-directing our passion to its proper end –Himself! With Christ at the center, Church says that the "law of the Gospel does not add new external precepts but proceeds to reform the heart, the root of human acts, where man chooses between the pure and impure."[8] All passion flows from the human heart. Therefore reforming the heart begins by re-directing those passions to Christ the perfect lover. Nature is God's first book: enjoy the goodness of creation – be it material things or persons but do not idolize them as if they are the source of goodness. Do not set your heart on them as the source of all your answers and happiness. This is called idolatry. No single creature in its beauty and goodness is meant to usurp the singular place and source of all Goodness, God Himself. Human beings alone are the only creatures *who can give VOICE to the whole of creation and sing this awesome truth.* St. Thomas sums it up well when speaking about the new Song we are called to sing with a new heart: "A song is the exultation of the mind dwelling on eternal things, bursting forth in the voice." Another word for this voice bursting into song is the unrestrained consuming love for God.

Often times we do not experience this incredible reality in order to voice its truth, in order to sing it out. We are blind. We are deaf to it. Bad decisions and a host of other things bring pain and hurt and can cause us to question God and our own self-worth. Yet John Paul II says that the heritage of our hearts is deeper than the sinfulness inherited. This means that there is a deep echo within us that says it is good to exist, it is good be here, it is good to be created male and female, it is good to want to love and be loved with a burning desire. In other words *I AM GOOD* by the grace of God. Despite the inheritance of my broken humanity so prone to selfishness, to see God more as an enemy than a friend, these deep echoes in my soul remind me that *I am indeed good* in His eyes: "My soul gives praise to the Lord; I will sing to the Lord all my days, make music to my God while I live" (Psalm 146). When we become aware of the "why" of this echo in us and learn to not block it out, but rather to receive his love, we hear the words: "I have loved you with an everlasting love" (Jeremiah 31,3).

What do I do with this wild passionate side of me? Direct it to Christ in the Paschal mystery. Look at the God-man, Jesus Christ, and how he loved us and gave himself up to death on the cross for love of humanity. It is in contemplating the pierced side of Christ that we discover the definition of true love. "In this contemplation [of the pierced side of Christ] the Christian discovers the path along which his life and love must move."[9] We call Christ's death on the

Cross, *the Passion*, because through this heroic transforming act of love he obediently took upon himself all the ugly, disordered misdirected passion in the human heart and gave us freedom from it. He gave us a new heart. "Contemplation of the self-donation of the son of God on the cross is the antidote to my own self-involvement. Contemplation is not simply meditating upon a narrative and marveling at its drama. Contemplation is that which heals a man and lets the living mystery of divine love affect the intellect and move the will to new life commitments."[10] If a person orders his desires and affections to the paschal mystery of Christ's unconditional love on the cross, disordered desires will be purified and authentic peace comes. The direct result from such prayer is the conviction: I *can* love passionately like Christ loved me.

The first numbers of the Catholic Catechism are about man's capacity for God. The only key that fits in the empty hole of my heart is the God-key. Made in his image and likeness, we have the capacity to receive his very Spirit in us, to share in his own blessed life. The Creator wants *to enter into* his creation-- to fill it with uncreated passionate life but he will not force himself on us. He asks permission. Was it not God's messenger Gabriel who came to Mary proposing God's plan, to allow the Holy Spirit to come upon her? Faith, in its deepest essence, is the openness of the human heart to the gift: to God's self-communication in the Holy Spirit.[11] To be open to the life of God is to be open to receive the intensity of that divine life, to be open to the action of God in you and around you and the communication of himself to you.   God gave us passion in our hearts because He is the source of all passion. He is Eros with a capital "E": primordial, heart-pulsating, passionate love, and, it is all of me that is the object of this Divine love. Yet Pope Benedict says that God's *eros* for man is also totally *agape,* that is, sacrificial love. Christianity does not demonize the human person but rather divinizes the human person. Divinization means participation in the inner life of God himself. What begins on earth will find its completion in heaven. This process of all consuming love, "of penetration and permeation of what is essentially human by what is essentially divine will then reach its peak so that the life of the human spirit will reach a fullness that was absolutely inaccessible to it before."[12] The starting point of all of this interior transformation begins when I encounter Christ. This encounter has the capacity to define me. Our true identity is given only by him. "It is Christ who reveals man to himself and makes his supreme calling clear."[13]

Questions for Group Discussion:

1. Why do I shy away from being passionate about having Christ in my life? What am I really passionate about? When will I fully accept that only God will bring true fulfillment in my life?

2. What examples of passion can I recall in the lives of the saints? What keeps me from following their examples? Am I afraid to face my deepest desires and the need to purify them to make them "all Christ's"?

3. What in my spiritual life seems inaccessible? What will it take to allow Christ to transform my life by passionately loving Him?

ENDNOTES

Dedication

[1] *Regnum Christi* is *Latin* for "Kingdom of Christ." See further historical background in Reflection IX.
[2] Pope John Paul II, *Mission of the Redeemer*, 86.

I. Unity and Charity

[3] Archbishop Stanislaw Rylko, "Ecclesial Movements and New Communities: The Response of the Holy Spirit to Today's Challenges of Evangelization," 5.

[4] Ibid., 3.
[5] Ibid., 4.
[6] Pope Francis, *Lumen Fidei*, 39.

II. What does "Kingdom" mean?

[1] CCC 363.
[2] Rylko, 8
[3] Cf. New Advent Catholic Encyclopedia, s.v. "Apostle".
[4] "The Movements know how to awaken a desire to 'make disciples' of Jesus Christ, a desire that often moves individuals, married couples, and even entire families to leave everything in order to embrace the mission," Rylko, 4.

III. Establishing the Kingdom of Christ

[1] Regnum Christi Handbook (RCHB), 25.

[2] CCC 1488.
[3] Cf. "Principles of the Charism of the Regnum Christi Movement," November 2012.
[4] J. Evert and B. Butler, *Theology of the Body for Teens,* (Ascension press, 2008), 33.

IV. Opposing the "kingdom of whatever"

[1] Cf. Brad Gregory, "The Unintended Reformation: How a Religious Revolution Secularized Society," Notre Dame, 2012.
[2] Thomas Dubay, *Faith and Certitude* (Ignatius Press), 12.
[3] CCC 357.
[4] John Cuddeback , *True Friendship, Where Virtue becomes Happiness* (Epic Press), 106-17.
[5] Ralph Martin, *The Fulfillment of All Desire: A Guidebook to God Based on the Wisdom of the Saints,* (Emmaus Road Publishing), 8.
[6] Denzinger, 301-302.
[7] *Oratio II contra Arianos,* 70: *PG* 26, 425 B, Saint Athanasius, "Man could not become divine remaining united to a creature, if the Son were not true God".
[7] RCHB, 16, 28-32
[8] Ibid.
[9] *Gaudium et Spes,* 22.
[10] RCHB, 3.
[11] Cf. Ibid, 74; See also 146.

V. Building the Kingdom of Christ through Communion

[1] Rylko, 3

[2] RCHB, 64.
[3] Ibid., 44.
[4] Ibid., 43.
[5] Rylko, 4.
[6] Ibid. 5.

VI. Core to the Kingdom: Militia Christi

[1] Thomas Dubay, *Faith and Certitude, 13.*

[2] John Paul II, *Redemptoris Hominis*, 10.

[3] "Communiqué of the Holy See regarding the Apostolic Visitation of the Congregation of the Legionaries of Christ," May 1, 2010.

[4] Fr Luis Garza, "Principal Traits of the Apostolic Charism of the Legion of Christ and Regnum Christi," (2011), 9.

[5] Communiqué..., May 1, 2010

[6] Cf. Homily of Pope Benedict XVI, October 26, 2011.

[7] Cf. Wednesday Audience of Benedict XVI, May 22, 2012.

[8] Rylko, 7.

[9] Rylko, 5.

[10] Cf. Ibid., 6.

[11] RCHB, 27.

VII. Forging an apostle of the Kingdom in Solitude

[1] CCC 355.

[2] RCHB 29: "Often they find that at a given point the road becomes uncertain, gradually they are let down in their false hopes, and disillusion, apathy and abandonment set in—a type of spiritual winter."

[3] Ibid.,121.

4 Cf. John Paul II , Man and Women He Created Them, A Theology of the Body, 11.1. The first part of the Pope's teaching is dedicated to three original human experiences in Genesis, one of which is original solitude. These experiences, "are always at the root of every human experience…Indeed, they are so interwoven with the ordinary things of life that we generally do not realize their extraordinary character."

[5] Ibid., 43,7.
[6] Ibid., 5,5.
[7] Ibid., 46, 5.
[8] Ibid.,55, 4.
[9] RCHB, 107.
[10] Ibid., 120.
[11] Ibid.
[12] Ibid., 110.

VIII. The Kingdom makes all things new:

[1] Ibid., 17.
[2] TOB, 32, 2
[3] Edward Leen, *The Holy Spirit (Scepter Press)*, 11.
[4] RCHB, 74.
[5] Ibid., 39.
[6] Ibid., 34.
[7] Romano Guardini, *La Coscienza* (Brescia, Italy, Morcelliana, 1961), 52.

IX. The Center piece of the Kingdom: The Sacred Heart

[1] Rylko, 2.
[2] RCHB, 75.
[3] St. Margaret Mary Alacoque, *Vie et Oeuvres* 2 (Paris,

1915), 321.

[4] Ibid.

[5] Cf. RCHB, 13 and 17

[6] Rylko, 5.

[7] RCHB, 27.

[8] Alacoque, 321.

[9] Rylko, 4.

[10] Ibid.

[11] Angelus Address of Pope John Paul II, June 24, 2002.

[12] Cf. RCHB, 175

[13] Angelus Address of Pope John Paul II, June 24th 2002.

X. A Kingdom of Desire: Passionate Love for Christ

[1] *Spe Salvi*, 47.

[2] RCHB, 33.

[3] Cantalamessa, *Agape and Eros*, 24.

[4] *Commentary on the Song of Songs*, St Gregory the Great.

[5] *Deus Caritas Est*, 4.

[6] Thomas Aquinas *Summa Theologiae* I-II.2.8.

[7] CCC 2338.

[8] CCC 1968.

[9] Deus Caritas Est, 12

[10] James Keating, "Christ Is the Sure Foundation: Priestly Human Formation Completed in and by Spiritual Formation," *Nova et Vetera,* (English Edition,Vol. 8, No. 4 (2010)), 889.

[11] *Dominum et Vivificantem*, 52

[12] TOB 67.3.

[13] *Gaudium et Spes*, 22.